# ORCAS

### SAM DRUMLIN

**PowerKiDS**
press.

New York

Published in 2013 by The Rosen Publishing Group, Inc.
29 East 21st Street, New York, NY 10010

First Edition

Editor: Amelie von Zumbusch
Book Design: Liz Gloor and Colleen Bialecki

Photo Credits: Cover Hyde John/Perspectives/Getty Images; p. 5 Xavier Marchant/Shutterstock.com; p. 7 © iStockphoto.com/Evgeniya Lazareva; p. 9 Kim Westerskov/Photographer's Choice/Getty Images; p. 11 Tom Middleton/Shutterstock.com; p. 13 Monika Wieland/Shutterstock.com; p. 15 Mike Price/Shutterstock.com; p. 17 Chris Cheadle/All Canada Photos/Getty Images; p. 19 Christian Musat/Shutterstock.com; p. 21 Jeroen van den Broek/Shutterstock.com; p. 23 David E. Myers/Stone/Getty Images; p. 24 iStockphoto/Thinkstock.

Library of Congress Cataloging-in-Publication Data

Drumlin, Sam.
  Orcas / by Sam Drumlin. — 1st ed.
     p. cm. — (Powerkids readers: sea friends)
  Includes index.
  ISBN 978-1-4488-9645-5 (library binding) — ISBN 978-1-4488-9748-3 (pbk.) —
  ISBN 978-1-4488-9749-0 (6-pack)
  1. Killer whale—Juvenile literature. I. Title.
  QL737.C432D787 2013
  599.53'6—dc23
                                        2012023594

Manufactured in the United States of America

CPSIA Compliance Information: Batch #W13PK3: For Further Information contact Rosen Publishing, New York, New York at 1-800-237-9932

# CONTENTS

Orcas are a kind of dolphin.

They are also called
killer whales.

They are big.

They **spy-hop** to look around.

11

Orcas are smart.

They can learn tricks.

They form groups, called **pods**.

Pods hunt together.

They eat many foods.

One **calf** is born at a time.

# WORDS TO KNOW

calf

pod

spy-hop

## INDEX

## WEBSITES

Due to the changing nature of Internet links, PowerKids Press has developed an online list of websites related to the subject of this book. This site is updated regularly. Please use this link to access the list:
www.powerkidslinks.com/pkrsf/whale/